AI Driven Product Management

INNOVATE WITH INTELLIGENCE

BY, HARDEEP SINGH

Preface

Over the past decade, I have dedicated my career to working in product teams, tirelessly analyzing vast amounts of customer data. My goal has always been to uncover themes, understand customer pain points, and identify key data points that drive product decisions. This manual process, while insightful, was incredibly time-consuming and often left me wishing for a more efficient way to extract meaningful insights.

The breakthrough came when I first experimented with AI tools to handle this analysis. To my astonishment, these tools not only saved me countless hours but also provided valuable insights from the vast data in no time. The efficiency and precision of AI in processing and interpreting data were nothing short of revolutionary.

Realizing the potential of AI-driven product management, I felt compelled to share this knowledge with the broader community. This book, "AI Driven Product Management," is the culmination of my experiences and discoveries. It aims to guide you through leveraging AI tools to optimize the product management lifecycle, enabling you to deliver greater value to your customers.

In this book, you will learn how AI can automatically recognize patterns and trends in your data, allowing you to make informed decisions quickly. You will discover how AI can enhance experimentation by rapidly identifying what works and implementing changes efficiently. Furthermore, I will show you how AI can streamline communication within your team by automating the creation of essential product documentation.

The integration of AI into product management is not about replacing the human touch but rather amplifying our capabilities. By freeing us from the mundane task of data analysis, AI empowers us to focus on strategic projects and innovation, ultimately driving better business outcomes and customer satisfaction.

I hope this book inspires you to embrace AI in your product management practices and unlock new levels of efficiency and insight. Thank you for joining me on this journey.

Sincerely,

Hardeep Singh

Table of Contents

INTRODUCTION

Chapter 1

Introduction to the AI Driven Product Management

Chapter 2

An overview of AI and product management

- Current state of AI in product management
- Product manager = AI product manager

Chapter 3

Embracing AI: Evolving your software strategy

- Decoding the revolutionary role of AI tools in product
- Shaping the right future strategy for AI
- Setting the stage with AI principles
- Crafting AI Driven Capabilities

Chapter 4

AI's role in product-led organizations

- What is a product-led organization?
- Advantages of AI in a product-led organization
- Expanding AI across teams in a product-led organization

Chapter 5

Amplifying product-led growth with AI

- Key pillars of product-led growth
- AI for creating free user experiences and "aha" moments
- Driving usability and stickiness with AI
- AI for driving purchases and virality

- Canva's success story: Fusing AI with PLG

Chapter 6

Making product development smarter

- Introduction to making product development smarter
- What is the Product Management Life Cycle?
- AI in the Discover phase
- AI in the Validate phase
- AI in the Build phase
- AI in the Launch phase
- AI in the Evaluate and Iterate phases

Conclusion

INTRODUCTION

In this book, I have discussed the use of AI tools in product management related activities that I have been doing to boost efficiency at work and come up with better use of my time on focusing more on the decision making rather than spending hours calculating and evaluating large data sets. Remember, AI is a product of numerous human minds, and while I personally believe that an AI cannot match a human's creative aspects and personas, I also do think that harnessing AI tools should be given a positive outlook in terms of workplace productivity.

I hope you enjoy this read.

Best Wishes,

Hardeep Singh

Chapter 1

Introduction to the AI for Product Management

Chapter 1

Introduction to the AI for Product Management

Welcome to the AI for Product Management ebook! These days, it's hard to go even a day without hearing or reading about AI. By now, it's clear that artificial intelligence will continue to transform the way we work, live, and interact. If you're a product manager or part of a product-led organization, you're probably curious about how this technology will shape the way you build, innovate, and bring software products to market.

Before we delve further into the topic, let's define artificial intelligence and explore some related terms. Artificial intelligence refers to the ability of machines to perform cognitive functions typically associated with human intelligence. AI is a broad discipline comprising various subfields, often referred to collectively as AI. However, understanding the distinctions is helpful. Let's take a quick overview of some types of AI that you'll encounter throughout this ebook.

Machine learning, for instance, focuses on using data and algorithms to mimic human learning and gradually improve accuracy. Instead of explicit programming, these algorithms detect patterns and make decisions based on data and experiences. Think of product recommendations on a retailer's website as an example of machine learning in action.

Deep learning, on the other hand, can process diverse data types like images, sound, and text, often yielding more accurate results than traditional machine learning. Companies developing driverless cars rely on deep learning algorithms to detect pedestrians, traffic signs, and objects.

Natural Language Processing (NLP) empowers machines to process and understand human language, enabling them to perform repetitive tasks like language translation, autocorrection, and acting as personal assistants on our phones.

Generative AI, a fascinating AI model, generates content in response to a prompt. Large Language Models (LLMs) are a popular type of generative AI. Trained on vast amounts of textual data, LLMs can generate anything from a report summary to a promotional email or even a chat with a friend. Examples of LLMs include ChatGPT and an AI model developed by a leading organization.

Although this ebook doesn't provide hands-on guidance on using AI tools for specific tasks, it will provide you with a clear understanding of how AI empowers product managers and product-led organizations. So, let's explore two ways you should view AI as a product manager.

First, AI is a tool that can help you build your product and improve internal processes. Second, AI can be a capability embedded in your product, offering AI-powered features that deliver value to users. While this ebook primarily focuses on the former, you'll also discover how to adapt your software strategy to incorporate AI functionality.

Since AI is a constantly evolving field with plenty to learn, a significant portion of this ebook will explore what's possible with AI and potential use cases that product and digital leaders can leverage. Speaking of possibilities, allow me to share an inspiring story. A few months ago, our CEO attended an event during the AI tools hype. A venture capitalist challenged the audience of executives to think beyond the initial application of generative AI. This VC encouraged them to consider how AI could have ten times the impact on the software they provide, creating exponential value for their customers. It's about making products exponentially better, not just incrementally. As a Product Management enthusiast, this idea stuck with me, highlighting the immense opportunity AI presents for product and digital teams to bring exponential positive impact to customers. If that's not the ultimate motivation for a product manager, I don't know what is.

However, it's important to acknowledge the fear that accompanies the rise of AI technology. AI introduces many unknowns about how to utilize it and what its ultimate outcomes will be. Fear of the unknown is natural to human nature. Interestingly, different groups exhibit varying levels of hesitancy toward AI. A recent study surveyed more than 1200 global companies in traditional businesses undergoing digital transformation. Unsurprisingly, the study found that a significant portion of company leaders ranked AI and machine learning skills as crucial for achieving business goals. However, contributors had mixed opinions on the prioritization of these skills. This discrepancy illustrates the current state of AI in the business world. While leadership is optimistic about AI, those individuals who will actually utilize the technology might not necessarily share the same sentiment. The fear I mentioned earlier plays a significant role in this discrepancy.

Recognizing this, I set out to create this ebook. My aim is to address these fears head-on and help product practitioners gain confidence in embracing AI. While there will always be more to learn in the coming months and years, my goal is to open your mind to AI and how you can leverage its power. By the end of this ebook, you'll be familiar with core AI use cases relevant to businesses with software and digital experiences. You'll also discover ways in which product managers can integrate AI as a strategic tool, not a threat. Furthermore, I have included real-world examples of AI-powered product development to help you identify specific ways to utilize AI in your own work. So, let's begin this exciting journey into the world of AI for product management!

Chapter 2

An overview of AI and Product Management

Chapter 2

An overview of AI and product management

Current state of AI in product management

At the end of this chapter, you will be able to:

1. Explain how AI can transform how product managers operate
2. Describe why product managers should view AI as a strategic tool
3. Identify key ways product managers can use AI in their work

We are at the beginning stages of a long journey with AI and product management. While it's exciting to consider the potential of AI in terms of speed and efficiency, let's start by understanding where we currently stand. Product managers will continue to perform their roles, but with AI as a tool to automate and expedite certain tasks. It's beneficial to view AI's role in product management in three main categories: data analysis, experimentation, and communication.

AI's Place in Building Products

In the realm of data analysis, product managers collect and analyze quantitative data such as product usage and user journeys, as well as qualitative data like customer feedback and open-text responses. AI plays a significant role here through pattern recognition using machine learning algorithms. Instead of spending time sifting through data and feedback, product managers can rely on AI to analyze and provide summaries. This aids in decision-making for product discovery, roadmap dynamics, and product-led growth strategies. With more data at their disposal, product managers can personalize the user experience by tailoring content, messaging, and workflows.

The second category, experimentation, becomes more accessible as AI reduces the time spent on data analysis.

Product managers will have more time for developing and conducting tests within the product. AI tools can suggest areas for multivariate feature testing and even run tests automatically. This approach to experimentation allows for rapid learning and implementation of changes.

Communication is the third category where AI can assist product managers. They are constantly communicating ideas, priorities, and plans, often with cross-functional teams. AI can automate the creation of user stories, persona descriptions, product requirements, release notes, and more. While AI technology streamlines communication tasks, product managers must maintain effective communication by being present and attentive to customers, engineers, stakeholders, and cross-functional teams. This is crucial for articulating value, validating problem-solving efforts, and providing necessary details for effective collaboration.

Two areas AI will enhance rather than replace

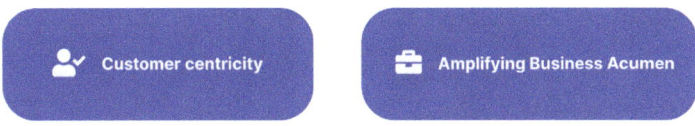

AI will amplify and enhance product management, not replace it. Being customer-centric and translating customer wants and needs into a product will remain a fundamental skill. Additionally, having a strong business sense is essential for making product decisions that align with company goals and strategic direction. AI can facilitate the creation of business cases, allowing product managers to focus on building better digital experiences.

It's important for product managers to embrace AI as a partner rather than a threat. AI frees up time for strategic projects and innovation, such as analyzing customer feedback and Net Promoter Score survey responses. By leveraging machine learning and feedback management software, product managers gain valuable hours to dedicate to increasing customer value.

Without Machine Learning	With Machine Learning
Manually comb through qualitative data	Spend less time analyzing qualitative data
Categorize data and analyze trends	Spend more time on strategic projects and innovation
Put together recommendations	

When considering AI's role in product management, we can draw parallels to previous technological advancements. Just as digital streaming revolutionized home entertainment and cloud computing transformed product delivery, AI empowers product managers to focus on rapid improvement and value creation. Similar to renewable energy's impact on reducing carbon footprints, the AI moment presents another opportunity for product managers to innovate for their customers' benefit.

Next, we'll explore specific ways that product managers can leverage AI to enhance their work.

Product Manager = AI Product Manager

AI has had a significant impact on product management, and it continues to shape the field in various ways. While there are dedicated AI product managers who specialize in using deep learning and machine learning, all product managers can benefit from developing AI skills. In fact, the modern product manager's objective is to drive business outcomes, and AI is an indispensable tool in achieving those goals efficiently.

Today there are

12000+

AI Product Manager Job Listings

AI tools have the power to cut through the noise in your data, providing valuable insights that may have been challenging to uncover manually. By automating workflows and streamlining processes, AI allows product managers to focus on delivering enhanced value to customers. It's important to note that AI is not a threat to the role of a product manager; instead, it represents a transformative change.

AI frees up product managers to deliver more value to customers.

Excitement surrounding the integration of AI into daily work is growing, even if it starts with small-scale implementations.

Let's explore some specific ways product managers can leverage AI both now and in the future.

Product Analytics

We'll begin with a broad use case: product analytics. Companies are increasingly adopting AI to boost productivity and achieve more with fewer resources. By harnessing AI alongside product analytics, product managers can sift through vast amounts of data, empowering them to make informed decisions. This democratization of data analysis helps extend the benefits of AI throughout the entire product team.

Customer feedback insights and NPS

While this opportunity is significant, a recent study reveals that only a fraction of product leaders currently leverage AI for data analysis. However, my advice is to start incorporating AI into product analytics, even if it's done gradually. Begin by focusing on a specific area or question that you want to explore. The tools and resources available to you will determine the scope of your implementation. For example, AI can be employed to expedite page and feature tracking in your product analytics platform, quickly identify user workflow issues, and extract key insights from customer feedback and NPS responses.

Another area where AI proves valuable is data quality analysis. Natural language processing algorithms can analyze user feedback and NPS responses related to specific features. This allows product managers to identify common pain points and themes, aiding in effective prioritization.

Product Roadmap optimization and feature prioritization

AI can also optimize the product roadmap by analyzing historical data and predicting the impact of specific features on metrics like retention, user satisfaction, and revenue. This data-driven approach assists product managers in making informed decisions about which features to prioritize.

User stories and persona creation

But AI's influence doesn't stop there; it can also be utilized during product planning by analyzing extensive data from multiple sources. It can generate user stories and personas, informed by product usage, market research, and user surveys.

Product Backlog management

AI can assist with backlog management, identifying valuable items, breaking them down into smaller tasks, and estimating effort.

In-app communication and copy creation

Lastly, generative AI plays a role in enhancing the end product experience. Whether it's providing in-app copy, crafting engaging UI messages, or automatically creating user guides, AI contributes to improving the overall user experience.

Although specific tools may not exist for each of these use cases, it's beneficial to consider the ways in which AI can enhance a product manager's effectiveness. By embracing AI, product managers can navigate their roles with greater efficiency, delivering exceptional value in the process.

Chapter 3

Embracing AI:

Evolving Your Software Strategy

Chapter 3

Embracing AI: Evolving your software strategy

Decoding the revolutionary role of AI tools in product

Today, the business world stands at a critical juncture. Digital experiences reign supreme, shaping customers' perceptions and ongoing engagement with brands across all industries. With the surge of generative AI technology, the pace of change is skyrocketing. But before forging ahead, let's pause to understand why AI tools are so transformative in product management.

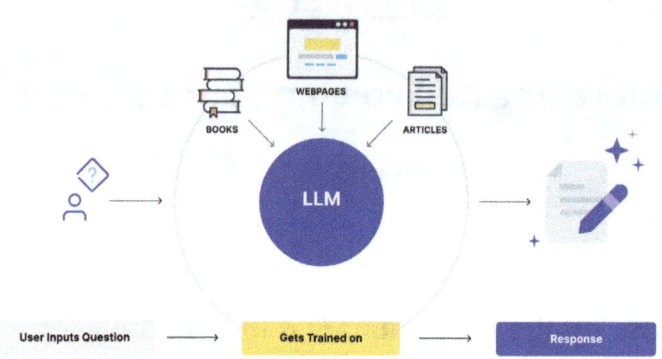

Take large language models (LLMs) like Chat GPT or Google's Bard, for example. These tools utilize deep learning algorithms to understand natural language and craft responses akin to human speech. Trained on a vast data set of internet text, they grasp intricate patterns and relationships among words. When users input queries, these tools draw from this wealth of knowledge to provide contextually relevant, grammatically correct, and engaging responses. Beyond language, similar technology finds application in diverse fields, from generating visual art to assisting developers in coding tasks.

For instance, in image generation, deep learning models can conjure realistic visuals based on textual descriptions.

In coding, they aid developers by suggesting code snippets or completions. Even in voice synthesis, they replicate human speech, enhancing interactions with technology. Such applications underscore the versatile potential of deep learning algorithms across various domains.

No doubt, AI holds the power to revolutionize how we interact with businesses and each other in the years ahead. Recall the impact of the iPhone. It transformed communication, media consumption, and information access, sparking a wave of innovation in mobile tech. Similarly, AI promises transformative change. Businesses must embrace this technology early to stay ahead, understanding its implications for software, digital experiences, and product strategies.

At its core, AI's abilities in pattern recognition and data analysis promise to redefine how product managers make decisions. Additionally, LLM technology can shape the end-user experience, facilitating self-service and enhancing support functions. Just as missing the mobile trend proved costly for some companies, failing to adapt to AI could have dire consequences. Thus, businesses must be vigilant as the AI era dawns.

In our next discussion, we'll delve into crafting the right AI strategy to navigate this evolving landscape.

Shaping the right future strategy for AI

In addition to product managers incorporating AI into their daily routines—something we'll delve into further in this book—AI also prompts a reevaluation of your overall software strategy. To aid in considering how AI might enhance your product's functionality, let's explore three crucial questions.

Question #1: What parts of your product need a makeover?

In the digital age of LLM AI tools, there's a clear opportunity to leverage them for quick, data-driven answers to users' inquiries. The goal is to eliminate cumbersome processes, where customers navigate through multiple steps and clicks. AI tools make information retrieval too convenient for outdated experiences to persist. Teams should begin by analyzing product analytics to pinpoint areas causing user frustration. These pain points are ripe for incorporating user-friendly question-answering features powered by LLMs. Though challenging, tailoring personalized interactive solutions like this is now essential.

For instance, Booking.com recognized a persistent friction point in its product: the search function. Customers often find themselves toggling between dates, destinations, and hotels to plan trips. With the emergence of LLM technology, Booking.com envisions optimizing this tedious process by introducing a natural language assistant. This assistant would streamline trip planning according to users' preferences, eliminating the need for excessive clicks.

Since identifying areas requiring change may not be immediately apparent, it's crucial to analyze usage and behavior data to understand the user experience fully.

Next, let's consider:

Question #2: What parts of your product will remain unchanged?

Just as certain areas of your product will benefit from AI-driven changes, there are also aspects that should remain untouched. Consider areas where users might prefer accessing information via dashboards or receiving insights through personalized charts, messages, or notifications. While AI will enhance these features by providing insights, they remain integral to your product.

Ultimately, while many product areas will evolve with AI, some will remain constant. Identifying these alongside areas needing change is crucial for refining your product roadmap.

Lastly, we have:

Question #3: What new features can AI enable?

While AI will undoubtedly impact existing products, it also opens doors to entirely new possibilities. Product teams now possess the means to creatively enhance user experiences and gain a competitive edge. Previously, AI was either absent or used to augment existing features. Now, teams can design entirely new experiences where AI takes the lead, supported by human input.

For instance, product managers can utilize AI to craft personalized onboarding processes, allowing users to provide context and adjust their experiences. In short, AI enables users to derive value from products more efficiently, resulting in heightened satisfaction.

Duolingo serves as a prime example of leveraging AI to introduce functionalities previously unattainable. By utilizing multimodal models, Duolingo introduced a subscription tier—Duolingo Max—with a role-playing feature allowing users to engage with AI characters. This feature addresses learners' needs by automatically providing explanations, enriching the learning experience.

Developing an AI strategy, once considered a luxury, is now imperative. It requires collaboration across various teams—product, engineering, UX, and machine learning. If executed wisely, these AI tools can exponentially improve customer experiences and business outcomes.

Setting the stage with AI Principles

AI is reshaping the business landscape in myriad ways, raising crucial ethical and practical concerns about its use.

As your organization navigates integrating AI into product management, it's vital to uphold commitments to customer privacy and security. One effective approach is to establish a set of AI principles to steer the use of artificial intelligence both internally and for customers. This ensures alignment across your product and engineering teams, providing a reference point for decision-making.

While working with an e-commerce firm, we developed eight guiding principles for our AI endeavors, which can serve as a useful starting point for others. Let's have a closer look into them:

Principle #1: Customer-Centric Approach

Our AI systems prioritize enhancing customer and end-user experiences through optimization, personalization, and usability improvements. Continuous feedback from customers informs the development of AI-powered features.

Principle #2: Transparency and Open Communication

We are committed to transparency in AI development and openly communicate with our community about the features we develop and deploy. Customers are informed about the capabilities and limitations of AI-powered functionalities.

Principle #3: Data Governance

We responsibly manage customer and user data throughout the AI model lifecycle, adhering to privacy rights, preferences, and industry-leading security standards.

Principle #4: Optionality and Customization

Customers retain control over their AI usage in our services, with features being optional and customizable to accommodate diverse needs and preferences.

Principle #5: Compliance with Legal and Regulatory Frameworks

We adhere to all applicable laws, regulations, and standards governing AI development and deployment, fostering a culture of legal and ethical responsibility.

Principle #6: Fairness and Equity

To ensure a fair product experience for all users, we actively mitigate potential biases throughout the model development lifecycle.

Principle #7: Thought Leadership

We strive to stay at the forefront of technological advancements, fostering a culture of continuous learning and exploration to become a leading voice in the industry.

Principle #8: Setting the Tone from the Top

Our executive team champions the implementation and adherence to these principles across all AI uses, services, and internal processes.

Once established, disseminating these principles to product, engineering, and company-wide teams ensures alignment and compliance. Engineers developing AI features refer to these guidelines, while the product team ensures alignment with company standards. While every organization's AI principles may vary, this framework provides a starting point for crafting clear guidelines around AI in product management.

Crafting AI Driven Capabilities

To begin our exploration of constructing AI-powered features, it's essential to understand the framework of "Four Levels of AI." Each level signifies a different degree of human versus AI involvement, offering valuable insights into the development of AI-driven functionality.

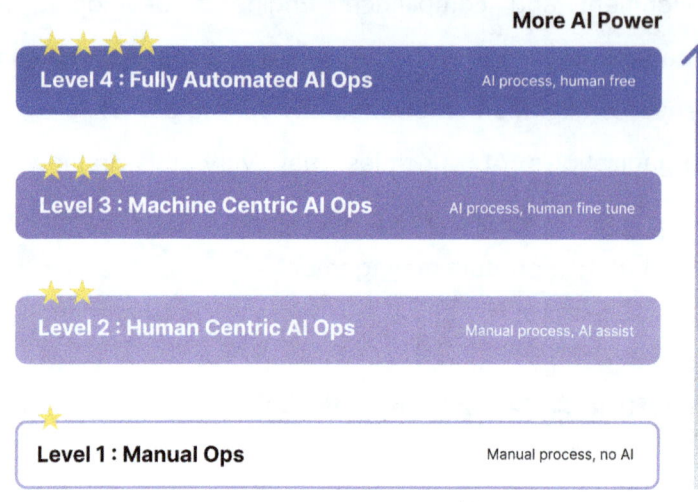

At the first level, human intervention is not involved. This was product management before AI's existence.

In the second level, human-driven processes are still there, but AI aids by offering insights and recommendations. Amazon's feature of summarizing product reviews is a great example of level two, where a human is buying a product and looking for honest reviews and recommendations. Instead of going through a lot of reviews, they can simply read an AI-generated summary.

Moving to the third level, AI assumes control of processes while humans refine, edit, or approve decisions. Netflix's onboarding experience illustrates this level, where AI curates personalized content(Homepage and other categories) based on user preferences, allowing users to make the final selection of content to watch.

Finally, at the fourth level, here, AI operates autonomously without human intervention, as it is in self-driving cars. In software development, product managers typically aim for levels two or three. Currently, the majority of AI features in development across most software companies align with level two. However, it's anticipated that more products will progress from level two to level three in the coming years.

As AI takes center stage in the business arena, many companies are exploring its potential to enhance products and customer experiences. While AI and machine learning offer vast possibilities, the success of AI features hinges largely on effective product management. Let's delve into three key reasons why:

Reason #1: Moving from level two to level three is a product question, not a machine learning question.

Elevating AI-powered features from level two to level three is primarily a product question, not solely a machine learning concern. Consider a recent project where our team aimed to develop an AI feature predicting business outcomes from product usage data. Initially, the feature operated at level two, providing insights. However, based on customer feedback, we recognized the need to elevate the functionality to level three, where users could act upon insights. This decision, driven by product managers and UX designers, underscores the pivotal role of product management in AI evolution.

Reason #2: Great AI Doesn't Guarantee a Great Product

Even if AI achieves 100% accuracy, a poor user experience diminishes product quality. Transparency, user intervention options, and feedback loops are crucial to ensuring AI-powered features enhance user experiences effectively. These considerations empower users and contribute to a superior product, irrespective of AI accuracy.

Reason #3: Product Manager Controls the Roadmap

Product managers control the product roadmap, balancing innovation with established plans. Despite capacity constraints, fostering an innovation culture, maintaining a balanced roadmap, and embracing unexpected changes are vital for accommodating AI-driven innovation.

As you embark on building AI features, remember these four tips:

Tip #1: Start Small and Focus on Value

Begin with level two AI features and gradually progress to higher levels while prioritizing value delivery to customers.

Tip #2: Form Working Groups

Assemble dedicated teams comprising engineers, data scientists, and designers to focus on building AI-powered products and features effectively.

Tip #3: Foster Innovation

Embrace a culture of experimentation and innovation, making room for AI-driven initiatives to flourish.

Tip #4: Embrace Feedback

Leverage early-stage feedback to refine AI algorithms continually, ensuring ongoing value delivery to customers.

Chapter 4

AI's Role in Product-led Organizations

Chapter 4

AI's Role in Product-led Organizations

What is a product-led organization?

A product-led organization is a company that focuses on its product, bringing all teams together to make the most of it. This helps them support and keep customers, manage costs, and achieve important goals.

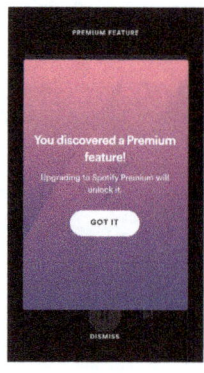
Premium Upgrade

New Features Walkthrough

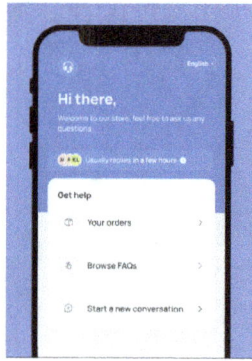
In-app Help

What does this look like in real life? Think of sales teams offering free trials of their software. Marketing teams showcasing new features within the product. Or support teams giving help within the app. These are all examples of how companies now interact with customers directly through their product. By doing this, they remove obstacles and make the product more appealing to users. But it doesn't stop there. Research shows that companies embracing these practices see more active users, more leads, and better revenue retention compared to others.

Impact of Product-led Practices

32% increase in total active users   **35%** more qualified leads   **18%** increase in net revenue retention

Let's explore six traits of product-led organizations:

Firstly, these companies align every part of their operation around the product. Instead of leaving product work to product and engineering teams alone, they involve everyone. They adjust their strategies based on how customers use the product. For instance, the customer success team might improve user onboarding, while marketing might use in-app messages to promote other products.

Secondly, product-led organizations rely on data rather than intuition. They constantly gather data on how people use the product. This helps them understand user needs and preferences better. By combining data with feedback from customers, they make informed decisions. Relying solely on intuition can be risky, especially as companies grow.

Thirdly, these companies use the product as a marketing tool. They communicate with customers through the product itself using in-app messages. This allows for real-time communication throughout the customer journey. It's effective for promoting events or updates, and it ensures information is shared in a way that's relevant to users.

Fourthly, product-led organizations prioritize onboarding experiences. They focus on making a great first impression and ensuring users understand how to use the product. They use in-app tools to create smooth onboarding processes that can be easily repeated. These experiences are personalized to suit different user needs.

Fifthly, these organizations empower users to find solutions on their own. They provide resources within the product, making it easy for users to help themselves. For example, they embed support documentation and useful resources within the product's navigation. This reduces the need for users to contact support for help.

Lastly, product-led organizations actively seek and use feedback from customers. They understand that user feedback is crucial for improving the product. They create processes to collect feedback and incorporate it into their roadmap and innovation strategy. This involves using in-app surveys, polls, and other tools to gather feedback directly from users.

Next, we'll explore how AI can further enhance the effectiveness of product-led organizations.

Advantages of AI in a product-led organization

Product-driven companies function differently compared to typical businesses. Instead of merely considering the product as something they create and sell, every department sees it as a way to engage with customers, gather data, and enhance the overall customer experience. It's because of these qualities that product-driven companies can uniquely benefit from artificial intelligence.

3 Advantages of AI for Product-led Companies

| Getting Smarter Exponentially | Helping Humans be more effective | Improving Product Delivery |

The advantages of AI in a product-driven organization can be grouped into three main categories. Firstly, AI helps these organizations become smarter. For a product-driven company to succeed, it needs a solid foundation of clean, accurate, and easily accessible data. AI aids in improving data-driven practices by helping to analyze data faster and more accurately than humans alone can manage. Secondly, AI assists humans in being more effective. Product-driven companies often delegate tasks to the product itself, such as onboarding, support, and sales interactions. With AI, teams can enhance these processes even further by automating repetitive tasks and workflows, allowing humans to focus on generating insights and taking action faster. Thirdly, AI contributes to improving product delivery. Product-driven organizations prioritize delivering value to users over simply shipping code. AI can support this goal by automating tasks like creating launch plans, analyzing qualitative data for feature improvements, and suggesting ways to iterate on products based on user adoption data.

Now, let's explore how AI can support each of the six characteristics of product-driven organizations. Firstly, these organizations align every function around the product. AI enables teams to analyze product data more efficiently, empowering them to make data-driven decisions across all departments. Secondly, product-driven companies prioritize data-driven decisions. AI and machine learning tools can process and organize vast amounts of data quickly, enabling companies to make faster and more informed decisions. Thirdly, these companies use the product as a marketing channel. AI helps personalize marketing efforts by analyzing product usage data and suggesting targeted communications for feature launches or promotions. Fourthly, product-driven organizations focus on providing excellent onboarding experiences. AI can analyze user behavior to personalize onboarding processes and suggest relevant features or content. Fifthly, these companies facilitate self-help for users. AI-powered chatbots and virtual assistants offer personalized support at scale, addressing common user queries and providing guidance within the product. Finally, product-driven organizations collect and utilize customer feedback. AI tools can analyze large volumes of feedback data to identify trends and suggest product improvements automatically.

These examples illustrate how AI seamlessly integrates into the core characteristics of a product-driven organization. In the next section, we'll explore how different teams within such organizations can leverage AI in their day-to-day work.

Expanding AI across teams in a product-led organization

By now, it should be evident that being product-led goes beyond just the product team. It's about the entire company coming together around the product, recognizing it as a tool to understand customers better and achieve key business goals. Similarly, AI has a role to play in every aspect of a product-led organization. Let's explore how three teams outside the product team can harness AI to advance their product-led initiatives.

Let's start with marketing. As mentioned earlier, one major advantage of AI is its ability to create personalized experiences on a large scale. Marketing teams can use AI tools to analyze product usage and customer feedback, gaining deeper insights into user needs and preferences. With this information, they can craft highly targeted in-app campaigns to drive feature adoption, webinar sign-ups, free trial conversions, and more. Product-led marketers also rely on product usage data and customer sentiment to identify power users and potential advocates, engaging with them to garner reviews or testimonials that boost product visibility. AI can expedite this analysis and even recommend which users have the potential to become power users, prompting the appropriate in-app outreach.

Moving on to sales teams, their use of AI revolves around driving growth. Product-led companies often offer free trials or freemium products to allow users to experience the product's value before committing to a purchase. Sales teams can leverage product usage data from these free and trial users to identify those most likely to upgrade to the premium product. However, determining which users to prioritize and when to reach out can be challenging. AI can assist sales teams by analyzing user behavior and identifying engagement patterns that signal high intent. Armed with this information, sales reps can focus their efforts on users with the highest likelihood of conversion and even use AI to craft personalized outreach messages.

Lastly, let's consider customer success. A key characteristic of product-led customer success teams is their data-driven approach to guiding customer interactions and proactively managing customer health. They use product analytics to track adoption and identify areas where customers may encounter difficulties, gathering feedback to gain deeper insights and context. Once again, AI can enhance these efforts by analyzing vast amounts of product usage data and customer feedback, quickly providing insights such as which customers are at risk of churn or which accounts are ripe for expansion. An AI-powered product experience platform could then automatically generate in-app guidance campaigns to drive conversion, expansion, or adoption. By automating such campaigns, customer success teams can allocate more time to strategic customer conversations or focus on accounts that require special attention, all while AI powers dynamic and targeted in-app campaigns in the background.

Considering how AI can support marketing, sales, and customer success teams, the potential for exponential impact becomes evident. In the future, organizations may even use AI to create a seamless product-led journey where marketing efforts inform sales experiences, which in turn shape the product experience, with data from all these interactions guiding customer success strategies. Though we're not there yet, it's exciting to contemplate the possibilities AI could unlock for product-led organizations in the future.

Chapter 5

Amplifying Product-led Growth with AI

Chapter 5

Amplifying Product-led Growth with AI

Key pillars of product-led growth

Product-led growth, often referred to as PLG, stands as a pivotal go-to-market strategy that places a company's software product at the forefront of the buying journey. This approach relies on the inherent value, features, performance, and virality of the product itself to drive much of the sales process. Considered as a key dimension within a product-led organization, PLG has rapidly gained traction across companies of varying sizes and industries. Instances of PLG in action include signing up for a product's free trial, inviting colleagues to utilize a tool already in use, or opting to upgrade to a premium version of a product with a credit card.

To delve into the discussion further, let's explore the six foundational pillars of product-led growth.

1. The first pillar revolves around offering a free user experience, marking the cornerstone of any substantive PLG strategy. This approach is rooted in the belief that the product serves as the most effective sales vehicle. Unlike cumbersome product demos and follow-up sequences, which consume valuable time from sales representatives and create friction for prospects, providing users with the opportunity to experience the product's value firsthand at their convenience proves more impactful. This can be achieved through free trials, which grant users access to the full functionality of the paid product for a limited time, or freemium products, offering a limited version of the product's functionality for free. Alternatively, product tours enable users to explore the application without necessitating sign-up.

2. The second pillar emphasizes delivering an "aha" moment as swiftly as possible upon user engagement. Products that drive successful PLG

are those that enable users to experience "aha" moments immediately, where they discover the key benefits of the product. Employing in-app guides that direct users to features or experiences leading to such moments proves particularly effective.

3. Third pillar is committing to best-in-class usability constitutes the third pillar. Designing the free product with optimized user experience (UX) and usability is crucial to guiding users towards "aha" moments seamlessly. Collecting feedback from users within the product, as they engage with it, helps ensure continuous improvements in usability.

4. The fourth pillar focuses on delighting users to foster stickiness. While achieving "aha" moments is essential, sustaining user engagement and retention requires ongoing efforts to keep users coming back for more. Robust feedback collection and analysis, coupled with quantitative usage data aid product teams in prioritizing features and functionalities.

5. The fifth pillar centers on making purchasing feel like a natural progression. Following repeated exposure to the value of the free product offering, users are primed for conversion. Forward-thinking product teams design free products that include key features while leaving others as part of the subscription model. Employing in-app notifications with clear calls to action (CTAs) can facilitate seamless transitions to the paid version.

6. Lastly, building in virality at every turn constitutes the sixth pillar of product-led growth. Distinguishing the best digital products is their ability to surprise and delight users, prompting them to become evangelists. Incorporating elements of virality into the product encourages users to spread the word, amplifying its reach and impact.

In essence, product-led growth enables companies to scale and grow efficiently by automating key functions across onboarding, support, sales, and marketing. This approach empowers customers and prospects to engage directly with the product, freeing up human resources to focus on strategic initiatives. Moreover, leveraging artificial intelligence (AI) can further optimize PLG efforts by enhancing automation, personalization, and data-driven decision-making.

In the subsequent discussion, we'll explore how product managers can leverage AI across each of the six pillars of PLG.

AI for creating free user experiences and "aha" moments

As we explore the foundational pillars of Product-Led Growth (PLG), it's crucial to emphasize the paramount importance of providing a seamless, free user experience. One of the remarkable strengths of AI lies in its adeptness at selectiveness of patterns within vast amounts of data, which is a skill highly desired by product managers eager to get actionable insights.

Consider the challenge of determining the optimal feature set for a freemium product. While the instinct may lean towards withholding premium features in the free version, an excessively stringent approach could hamper user adoption and hinder growth. Striking the delicate balance of offering value while enticing users to explore premium features is where the crux lies.

This is where AI comes into play. By harnessing AI-powered analytics, product managers can delve into data from paid products, identifying usage patterns and correlating them with user engagement metrics. This invaluable insight enables them to pinpoint the features most likely to resonate with free users, thereby enhancing the overall user experience and fostering conversion.

Moreover, AI holds the promise of proactively flagging invaluable insights, such as identifying user behaviors indicative of long-term engagement and recommending strategies to optimize user retention and drive growth.

Looking ahead, as the advent of generative AI looms on the horizon, the significance of offering free product tiers within a comprehensive PLG strategy cannot be overstated. With the proliferation of AI-driven outreach methods, traditional channels risk becoming saturated, rendering it increasingly challenging for companies to cut through the noise and connect with potential prospects.

In such a landscape, providing a compelling value proposition through free products emerges as a strategic imperative. By allowing prospects to experience the tangible benefits of their offerings firsthand, companies can effectively showcase the value proposition and nurture deeper engagement - a feat that AI-fueled analytics can help streamline and optimize.

Transitioning to the second pillar of PLG, the focus shifts to delivering the coveted "aha" moment - the instant of vision where users grasp the full extent of a product's value proposition. While these moments wield immense transformative potential, engineering them is no trivial task. They must resonate deeply with users, eliciting a sense of revelation or understanding that compels them to further explore the product's offerings.

Herein lies another arena where AI shines. By leveraging AI-driven analytics, product managers can sift through vast repositories of user data, identifying usage patterns, and discerning correlations between specific user behaviors and subsequent conversions or upsells. Armed with this wealth of insights, product managers can strategically craft and refine onboarding experiences, ensuring that users are seamlessly guided towards these pivotal "aha" moments.

Furthermore, personalization emerges as a potent tool for enhancing user engagement and driving conversion. Recognizing that different user segments possess unique needs and preferences, AI enables product managers to tailor the user experience with surgical precision. Whether it's customizing feature recommendations or crafting targeted messaging, AI empowers product teams to deliver personalized experiences that resonate deeply with users, thereby accelerating the journey towards the coveted "aha" moment.

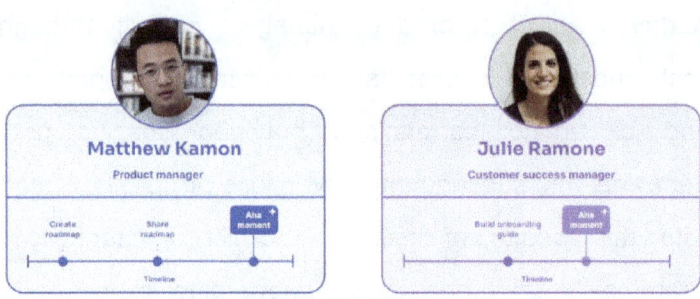

In essence, AI serves as a formidable ally in the pursuit of Product-Led Growth, enabling product managers to navigate the intricacies of modern user acquisition and retention strategies with unparalleled precision and efficacy. As the digital landscape continues to evolve and innovate, the integration of AI-driven analytics and personalization technologies will remain indispensable for organizations seeking to thrive in an increasingly competitive marketplace.

By harnessing the power of AI, product managers can unlock a treasure trove of insights, optimize user experiences, and drive sustained growth—all while staying one step ahead of the curve in an ever-evolving digital ecosystem.

This transformative potential underscores the pivotal role that AI plays in shaping the future of product management and underscores the imperative for organizations to embrace AI-driven strategies as they chart their course towards sustained success and growth in the digital age.

Driving usability and stickiness with AI

In the realm of Product-Led Growth (PLG), the third pillar emphasizes achieving top-tier usability, presenting numerous opportunities for AI integration. Let's delve into the various ways AI can transform usability.

AI's ability to rapidly analyze vast datasets is key. Through an AI-powered product experience platform, we can identify user friction points and even automatically suggest resources based on their behavior. Advanced tools may track user resource selections to refine future recommendations, profoundly enhancing the user experience.

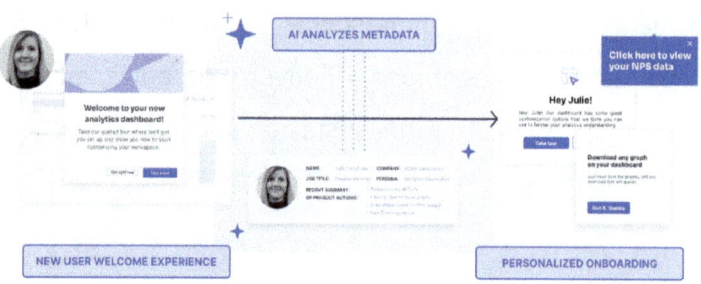

Another significant application of AI in enhancing usability is in onboarding processes. By leveraging AI's power, product managers can craft hyper-specific onboarding flows tailored to users' needs. This ensures that every user receives a personalized first experience with the product, a crucial aspect of driving virality and engagement.

Moreover, AI unlocks powerful opportunities for increasing usability.

Today, users expect consumer-level experiences from all softwares, including B2B applications.

With AI and natural language capabilities, product managers can bridge this expectation gap. For instance, in a rental car app, users could simply describe their desired trip using natural language, streamlining the input process.

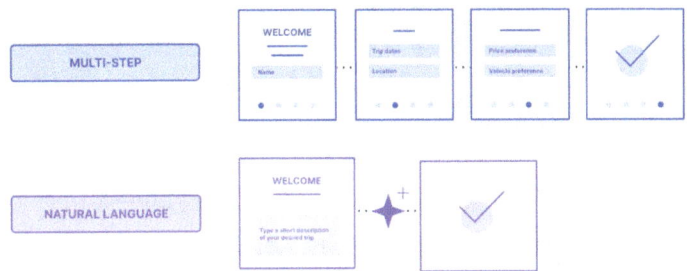

Looking ahead, there's immense potential for AI to further empower product managers. Imagine a future where product managers can effortlessly query product data or build segments using natural language - a prospect that promises to revolutionize product management tasks.

Now, let's transition to the fourth pillar of PLG - delighting users to encourage stickiness. Collecting and acting on feedback is essential for driving product-led growth. Here, AI proves invaluable by helping product managers sift through and derive insights from vast amounts of feedback data. AI tools categorize feedback into actionable themes and, combined with product usage data, pinpoint areas for improvement or feature prioritization.

A successful PLG strategy hinges on speed and agility. AI facilitates rapid testing, measurement of success, and iterative improvements by leveraging feedback effectively. By harnessing AI-driven insights, product managers can ensure they're building features and functionality that keep users coming back.

In summary, AI serves as a catalyst for revolutionizing usability and enhancing user delight in product management. Its integration not only enriches the user experience but also drives sustained growth and fosters enduring user loyalty. As we continue to leverage the power of AI, the possibilities for innovation and advancement in product management are boundless.

This comprehensive approach to usability, combined with AI-driven insights, propels product-led growth strategies to new heights. By embracing AI, product managers can stay ahead of the curve and lead their organizations to success in today's rapidly evolving digital landscape.

AI for driving purchases and virality

Let's delve into the fifth pillar of PLG, which revolves around making purchasing feel like the natural next step. As discussed earlier, leveraging in-app notifications is a powerful approach to address this pillar, guiding users towards making purchases at the opportune moments in their journey. With AI, product managers can enhance the effectiveness of these in-app messages. By analyzing usage data from free products, along with NPS, feedback, and past conversion data, AI can identify ripe moments for prompting purchases that may have otherwise been overlooked. Advanced AI tools can even automatically generate these in-app guides, allowing for quick review, editing, and deployment.

Moreover, AI and machine learning algorithms can analyze user behavior, company characteristics, and purchase patterns to offer personalized product recommendations. By exposing users to additional functionality tailored to their specific needs, AI increases the likelihood of conversion. Additionally, AI plays a role in pricing and packaging strategies, which directly influence purchasing decisions. Product managers can leverage AI to conduct extensive tests on pricing, packaging, and coupons, optimizing their PLG motion. Similar to onboarding, AI's ability to rapidly analyze vast amounts of data enables personalized and dynamic pricing based on factors like user location, company size, and time of year.

Moving on to the sixth PLG pillar - building in virality at every turn. Unlike the traditional purchasing funnel, PLG relies on viral growth loops, also known as the flywheel model. Calendly, the meeting scheduling platform, exemplifies this concept. After signing up for Calendly, users create meeting scheduling links to share with invitees. As events are scheduled and accepted, users are prompted to sign up for Calendly themselves, naturally propagating the product to their colleagues and peers.

Similar to the previous pillars, AI can assist product managers in analyzing behavior data to pinpoint optimal moments for users to share the product within their workflows. Utilizing generative AI, product managers can create in-app content to encourage sharing and collaboration. While identifying the inherent virality of a product remains the responsibility of the product manager, AI tools expedite the process of obtaining insights and implementing virality tactics.

In summary, AI serves as a valuable asset in optimizing both the purchasing experience and virality aspects of PLG strategies. By leveraging AI-driven insights, product managers can enhance user engagement, increase conversion rates, and foster organic growth within their user base.

Canva's success story: Combining AI with PLG

Product managers today harness the power of AI not only behind the scenes but also in delivering AI-driven capabilities directly to users. Let's explore a real-world example of how AI and product-led growth converge in Canva, a widely-used graphic design platform.

Canva recently unveiled "Magic Design," an AI-driven feature designed to assist users in various design tasks, including presentations, social media graphics, posters, videos, logos, and more. This innovative tool not only handles design layout but also aids in crafting content. By swiftly providing well-designed and on-point content, Canva's Magic Design tool effectively delivers value to users, leading them to an "aha" moment, all within a free user experience. These outcomes align perfectly with the core pillars of product-led growth, emphasizing the importance of delivering immediate value and nurturing user engagement.

Beyond its core functionality, Canva's Magic Design feature also plays a pivotal role in user conversion. Instead of employing traditional push tactics, Canva adopts a more nuanced approach. For instance, when users attempt to export their decks, Canva doesn't immediately prompt them to upgrade to a paid plan. Instead, users are presented with choices. They can opt to share their deck for free with watermarks on images, pay a one-time fee to remove watermarks, or subscribe to Canva's pro plan for continuous access to an extensive image library. By providing users with these options, Canva empowers them to make informed decisions, ensuring that transitioning to a paid plan feels like a natural progression rather than a forced upgrade.

Moreover, Canva recognizes the viral potential inherent in its Magic Design feature. Leveraging AI-driven insights, Canva facilitates seamless collaboration and sharing among users. Through clear prompts for link sharing and invitations, Canva encourages delighted users to spread the word, thereby fostering organic growth and product-led expansion.

In the broader context of product management, AI is not seen as a replacement for human creativity but rather as a complement that enhances it. AI-driven features within a PLG framework serve to delight users, drive conversions, and ultimately yield superior business outcomes. Canva's strategic integration of AI exemplifies how technology can serve as a catalyst for growth while maintaining a user-centric approach.

In conclusion, Canva's innovative use of AI within a product-led growth framework exemplifies the symbiotic relationship between technology and user experience. By leveraging AI to deliver immediate value, empower users, and foster virality, Canva sets a high standard for companies seeking to thrive in today's digital landscape. As the role of AI continues to evolve, product managers must remain adaptive and innovative, leveraging technology to create seamless, engaging experiences that drive sustained growth and customer satisfaction.

Chapter 6

Making Product Development Smarter

Chapter 6

Making product development smarter

Being a product manager involves grappling with the challenge of deciding what features to prioritize and build. While AI won't make these decisions for you, it can certainly lend a helping hand by providing valuable insights to expedite and enhance your decision-making process. In this discussion, we'll explore how AI can be integrated into each stage of the product management life cycle, offering practical guidance and real-world examples along the way.

Going further, we'll delve into the various phases of the product management life cycle and highlight how AI can play a role or potentially play a role in each stage. By the end of our exploration, you'll gain a deeper understanding of how AI can be applied at different points in the product life cycle. Moreover, you'll be equipped to develop a strategic plan for incorporating AI into your product development process, ensuring efficiency and effectiveness every step of the way.

What is the Product Management Life Cycle?

Before delving into AI's role, let's first clarify what the product management life cycle entails. It's essentially a data-driven approach that empowers product managers to prioritize business outcomes over simply pushing out features, making it an ideal arena for AI applications.

At its core, the product management life cycle is a cyclical framework guiding the development and enhancement of successful products. Let's take a brief look at each of its six phases.

Phase zero

Known as "Define a business outcome," serves as the starting point by establishing a clear business objective for product development. This ensures that efforts remain aligned with the overarching goals of the company.

Phase 1 - Discover

Product managers focus on identifying the desired outcome and understanding the obstacles hindering its achievement. This involves exploring questions such as "What challenges are preventing customer retention?" and "What factors are impeding adoption?"

Phase 2 - Validate

"Validate," entails collecting data to ensure that proposed solutions effectively address identified problems. This phase aims to validate product ideas and determine the most viable solutions to pursue.

Phase 3 - Build

Engineers commence development based on agreed-upon solutions. Product managers collaborate closely with engineers and designers to ensure that the envisioned idea is brought to life as intended. This phase also involves sharing and adjusting the product roadmap as necessary.

Phase 4 - Launch

It's time to introduce your new functionality to the world and ensure that customers adopt and continue using it. During this phase, collaboration with marketing, customer success, and sales teams is crucial to develop a comprehensive go-to-market plan that resonates with your target audience and influences their behavior.

Phase 5 - Evaluate

Evaluate follows the launch of a new product or feature. It's essential to assess its success using both quantitative and qualitative data to gauge its impact and effectiveness.

Phase 6 - Iterate

Iterate happens shortly after data collection and analysis begin. In this phase, the focus shifts to iteration mode, where you identify opportunities for improvement and refine what you've built. This marks the beginning of another cycle of the lifecycle as you circle back to product discovery.

The inherent value of this product management lifecycle version lies in its ability to help companies optimize their R&D expenditure. When executed effectively, product managers gain confidence in decision-making, leading to better allocation of resources and enhanced productivity within the product team. Moreover, for larger, more traditional companies, this framework facilitates the modernization of digital product development practices and fosters the evolution of sophisticated product organizations. The product management life cycle framework offers numerous opportunities for product managers to leverage AI, further enhancing efficiency and effectiveness.

Next, we'll delve into how AI can be integrated at each phase of the lifecycle, exploring its potential impact and benefits.

AI in the Discover phase

In successfully navigating the Discovery phase, it boils down to grasping both user pain points and broader market dynamics. This involves posing pertinent questions aligned with desired business outcomes. For instance:

- What do typical user flows look like?

- What's stopping users who are churned from achieving their goals?

- Are there specific workflows where churned users frequently encounter obstacles?

- What trends emerge from user feedback, and how effectively is that feedback addressed?

- **How do highly satisfied or "power users" typically engage with the product?**

Traditionally, product managers had to manually analyze a plethora of qualitative and quantitative data to find answers. However, with the advent of AI tools, they can now obtain concrete insights, discern meaningful patterns amidst the noise, and receive recommendations on the best path forward at an unprecedented scale.

Effective Discovery necessitates data from diverse sources, spanning customer support tickets, user interviews, sales and support calls, NPS surveys, customer feedback, and product usage metrics. AI streamlines this process by synthesizing and identifying patterns across multiple data sources, thereby empowering product managers to fuel their Discovery efforts with a wealth of insights. Moreover, AI tools can generate actionable recommendations and evidence to substantiate proposed user problems, enriching the Discovery phase and bolstering the confidence of product managers in their findings.

Consider the scenario of enhancing retention, as previously discussed. Initially, you might explore the disparity in usage between retained and non-retained users. Instead of manually sifting through product usage data, an AI-driven product analytics tool can swiftly analyze data and extract insights. It can address queries such as: What features are predominantly used by retained customers? And do these usage patterns extend across the broader user base?

Perhaps, your AI tool reveals that retained users consistently complete a new dashboard creation workflow within their first month of product usage. This prompt insight allows for a deeper dive into the journey of churned users through this workflow. AI can analyze this data as well, pinpointing crucial friction points that necessitate attention. Simultaneously, AI aids product managers in effectively combining quantitative usage data with qualitative feedback from various sources.

For instance, your product experience platform could automatically aggregate feedback related to specific product areas or workflow queries. This showcases just a fraction of AI's potential in the Discovery phase of the product management lifecycle. Ultimately, AI enables product managers to analyze extensive data sets, facilitating quicker and more informed decision-making, thus propelling them forward into the subsequent phase - Validate.

AI in the Validate phase

In the Discover phase, identifying multiple solutions to address user pain points is common. However, determining the optimal solution – one that maximizes both customer satisfaction and business ROI – is crucial. This is where the Validate phase steps in, and with AI, product managers gain unprecedented confidence in their decision-making process. Historically, validation has been a time-consuming endeavor, often tempting product managers to rush through it or skip it altogether, risking the development of the wrong product.

Traditionally, validation involved conducting one-on-one interviews with customers, presenting proposed solutions, and gathering feedback. Subsequently, product managers faced the challenge of synthesizing and analyzing this feedback to identify prevalent themes and prioritize solutions. Recently, product managers have expanded validation efforts by integrating data from various sources, including product usage data, in-app polls, surveys, and support tickets. However, the sheer volume of data poses a significant challenge in terms of analysis and actionable insights.

AI-powered tools offer a solution by enabling rapid analysis of data across multiple channels and providing data-driven recommendations. Additionally, validation often entails testing prototypes with users to gather initial feedback before proceeding with full-scale development. AI facilitates this process by expediting prototype development through generative AI, which uses prompts and customer data to quickly generate prototypes ready for validation.

For instance, product managers can leverage generative AI to provide prompts and customer data, resulting in prototypes ready for validation. Moreover, AI empowers product managers to test multiple prototypes simultaneously, accelerating the validation process and instilling confidence before engineers commence full-scale development. This seamless integration of AI into the validation phase streamlines decision-making and enhances the overall product management lifecycle, paving the way for the subsequent phase – Build.

AI in the Build phase

During the build phase, AI serves as a valuable asset for product managers, particularly in product testing. By leveraging AI, product managers can integrate testing into their roadmap earlier, saving valuable time. AI tools can analyze the product's code base and swiftly suggest how feature changes will impact the overall product, streamlining the testing process.

Additionally, product managers often find themselves gathering various types of documentation for engineering and design teams to guide the building process. These include user stories, product requirements documents (PRDs), and acceptance criteria. User stories outline product or feature requirements from the perspective of user value, while PRDs detail necessary capabilities for design and development teams. Acceptance criteria define the conditions a product or feature must meet for user acceptance.

With AI assistance, product managers can expedite this documentation process, which is typically manual and time-consuming. Instead of drafting entire user stories and acceptance criteria from scratch, product managers can input brief descriptions into AI tools, which generate the documents for editing. Similarly, AI can generate PRDs based on stored data about the product and its users, allowing product managers to focus on refining the details.

Moreover, AI enables product managers to handle version control and documentation effectively. With numerous teams collaborating on the same project, version control ensures that everyone is working on the latest iteration, preventing confusion and minimizing errors. AI-powered tools can automate version control processes, reducing the risk of inconsistencies and ensuring seamless collaboration.

Furthermore, AI facilitates data-driven decision-making during the build phase. By analyzing vast amounts of data from various sources, including user feedback, market trends, and competitor insights, AI provides valuable insights to guide product development. Product managers can use AI-generated analytics to identify patterns, anticipate user needs, and prioritize features based on their impact on user satisfaction and business goals.

As AI empowers product managers to build, test, and release functionality more efficiently, the frequency of product launches increases. This acceleration means that product managers can execute launches of all sizes more frequently, driving continuous improvement and innovation.

In conclusion, AI plays a crucial role in enhancing the build phase of the product management lifecycle. By streamlining testing processes, expediting documentation, enabling effective version control, and facilitating data-driven decision-making, AI empowers product managers to deliver high-quality products efficiently. In the upcoming discussion, we'll explore how AI contributes to the fourth phase of the product management lifecycle — Launch.

AI in the Launch phase

As agile methodologies and continuous delivery practices have gained traction, R&D teams now prioritize incremental software releases to specific user segments over time, rather than large, one-time launches. This shift towards iterative releases demands a more strategic approach to product launches. Product managers collaborate closely with sales and marketing teams to ensure optimal reach to target customers and prospects. They provide guidance on launch timing and feature positioning, making decisions on which features should be monetized to maximize conversion and retention rates.

In today's landscape, launches are more frequent but smaller in scale, prompting product managers to employ in-app guides and walkthroughs to announce releases and encourage feature adoption. These personalized guides enhance the user experience by guiding users through new functionality. However, the integration of AI tools takes user-centric launches to a new level. AI empowers product managers to tailor releases based on user preferences and behavior, ensuring that launches are more targeted and effective.

With AI assistance, product managers can deliver releases that resonate with users on a deeper level, increasing the likelihood of adoption and satisfaction. By leveraging AI-driven insights, product managers can optimize the launch process, driving better outcomes for both users and the business. Ultimately, AI enables product managers to navigate the complexities of modern product launches with greater precision and efficiency, resulting in enhanced user experiences and improved product performance.

With the advent of AI technology, product managers are stepping away from manual release scheduling towards smarter, data-driven release strategies. These intelligent releases involve a gradual rollout of both the product or feature itself and its accompanying promotional content, all guided by user usage patterns and feedback. Leveraging AI's capacity to analyze vast datasets, product managers can efficiently navigate this process.

Through AI-driven launch processes, product managers gain access to automated dashboards and reports that track key metrics and goals. These insights, generated in real-time, allow them to monitor adoption rates and assess the impact of releases on critical business outcomes like revenue growth and churn reduction. Moreover, AI facilitates the implementation of product-led growth strategies, enabling personalized user experiences tailored to individual characteristics and usage patterns.

By utilizing AI-powered product experience tools, product managers can identify opportune moments to showcase new products or features to users, guiding them along their adoption journey. Through targeted in-app messaging, users can be nudged towards adopting paid products at the most suitable times, optimizing conversion rates.

However, launching a product is just the beginning of the journey. Product managers must then shift their focus to evaluating adoption rates, monitoring user behavior, and identifying areas for improvement. This transition marks the transition to the final phases of the product management lifecycle: Evaluate and Iterate. In these phases, product managers leverage AI-driven insights to refine and enhance their products continuously.

AI in the Evaluate and Iterate phases

A new product or feature rollout doesn't end with a go live. In order to ensure continued success, product managers need to evaluate what resonated and working about a release and what isn't. This requires analyzing product usage data, going through user feedback and seeing whether support tickets are coming in tied to a release, and if so, what's generating them?

During the evaluate phase zooming in on both product usage data and customer feedback is key to getting insights into user behavior, where people may be getting stuck or what action users are or aren't taking. In a similar way, analyzing feedback and NPS data gives product managers a sense of whether they've solved problems identified during Discovery. AI can radically optimize this work by auto determining what is and what isn't working about the new product or feature, and then giving product managers recommendations on what to do next.

AI-powered product analytics and feedback management tools can analyze this quantitative and qualitative data on a scale and at a speed humans couldn't do on their own. From there, the right AI tools can even create dashboards for product managers to monitor and measure release performance with business outcomes and goals. This is a great example of AI empowering product managers, not replacing them. With AI, product managers can more quickly and efficiently evaluate the success of a release, accelerating their ability to identify and implement improvements.

In the final phase of the product management lifecycle, iterate, product managers must come back to the question of whether a new product or feature generated the desired business outcome. If it didn't and even if it did, chances are you will be iterating to improve the product and achieve even better business results. As product managers iterate and figure out what improvements to prioritize. AI will once again prove transformative throughout each phase of the life cycle.

Conclusion

As we discuss throughout this book, there is a huge opportunity for product managers to leverage AI at every step of the product management lifecycle. More importantly, AI will accelerate a pre-existing trend in product teams.

The product manager of the future will be measured by business outcomes achieved rather than mere features shipped.

AI will do this not by replacing product managers, but by augmenting their capabilities for analyzing data, forming recommendations and taking the right actions. As a product manager myself, I'm excited to see how AI will usher in a new chapter in product management, where product managers are freed up to be more creative, build more and better and see their creations through to a business impact never before possible.

www.ingramcontent.com/pod-product-compliance
Lightning Source LLC
Chambersburg PA
CBHW070310230526
45470CB00002B/800